Copyright © 2022 by Im Just Here To Make You Think Inc. and Dane Calloway and Taneisha Calloway. All rights reserved.

Published by Mr. & Mrs. Calloway Inc.
www.imjusttheretomakeyouthink.com

In Loving Memory

Of

Our Indigenous Ancestors

Dorothea Williamson

Cynthia Robinson

Freddy Williamson

Rhoda Calloway

Clara Russell

Roslyn Cross

Dedicated To The Niijis Of Turtle Island And Our Ancestors Respectfully

Thank you all that has been supporting me over the years with your much-appreciated contributions towards me, my cause, and the content that I present to the public because that enables me to continuously present this publicly verifiable evidence of documentation concerning various parts of our history to you guys, along with traveling and video documenting places or areas that most of you may not have witnessed yet.

Thank you so very much for your continued support.

And a very special thank you to my beautiful wife, Taneisha Calloway, for putting up with these long hours of researching with me, and me being a headache at times, while also managing the duties of being my wife and the mother of our beautiful children. Wado, my love, it's been seventeen years now and we are and will continue to go strong together. - Dane Calloway

It Was Told In Reverse

The Untold Truth About The Transatlantic Slave Trade

By Dane and Taneisha Calloway

Table of Contents

Preface xi

Chapter One: The Introduction Of The Gospel 1

Chapter Two: The Starving Time 11

Chapter Three: 20 And Odd Negras 23

Chapter Four: To Immigrate And To Emigrate (Prisoners of War) 43

Chapter Five: Removing The Negro Population 48

Chapter Six: Immigrating The Negro 56

Chapter Seven: The Establishment Of The American Society For Colonizing The

Free People Of Color In The United States Of America 62

Chapter Eight: The Correlation Between Africans And American Indians 72

Chapter Nine: The Indians Are The Niiji 77

Chapter Ten: The Agenda Of The American Colonization Society............. 89

Chapter Eleven: Paper Genocide 95

Chapter Twelve: The Indian Wars That Led To White Tears 105

Chapter Thirteen: Sent To Africa, Not From Africa 113

Chapter Fourteen: Factors Of Expatriation 119

Bibliography 128

More About The Author 136

Preface

Incoming immigrants with the desire to become leading American colonizationalists later recognized that compulsory education was one of the most successful social engineering experiments that influenced public perception and beliefs, to suit the purposes of justifying their heartless actions of land-grabbing, identify-theft, industrialism, racism, and systematic indoctrination just to name a few things, all favoring their newly established independent foreign government.

Ever since the inception and implementation of compulsory education during the early 1900s, the Niiji were forced to learn strict curriculums concerning their history especially, in a one-directional formatted belief system initially conducted by prominent foreign dictators of American policies.

These prominent foreign individuals had an idea to teach the Niiji their malicious propaganda of indoctrination, to not only decimate the Niiji's literacy but also ensure that our ancestor's ancient history here in America had been totally erased from their mindsets, and even from common knowledge, by the use of fictional storytelling.

One of the multiple fictional stories taught throughout school history curriculums and their associated programs was an error-filled modified version of the Middle Passage story, known today as the Transatlantic slave trade.

The early 1900s carried a flux of government-funded groups or organizations that heavily persuaded the idea of teaching the Niiji that their history was somehow "written by the victors", and that the foreign writers of this history would know best as to what exactly occurred throughout these lands during the existence of America in general, and even before the foreigner's arrival.

This manifests a ball of confusion, and another fact or issue rather points out, that no one has ever thought about challenging the education that was vigorously given to them.

And I said vigorously, because, did you want to learn the things that you were taught in school, or were you given no choice?

That is called indoctrination by the way, which means "to often repeat an idea or belief to someone, until they accept it, without criticism or question."

This explains why most teachers or college/university professors do not care to hear multiple direct questions from you, because that tends to reveal that you could be a so-called troublemaker, and you may be disrupting the flow of the class, just by simply asking questions concerning the authenticity of, for example, the history that was forcefully given to you to learn about.

But that also exposes the hidden manipulative agenda of indoctrination and all conspiracies within it, in which no one dares to question it, and that is exactly what these groups or organizations, who are funded by the government, are counting on. Your ignorance.

Which is defined as a lack of knowledge. When you see the word ignorance, you can pinpoint that it is derived from the word ignore, which means "to refuse to take notice of or acknowledge", and acknowledge means "to accept or admit the existence or truth of".

So in other words, the government is strictly counting on you not knowing the truth, and whenever you decide to conduct actual research, they will not only conceal the truth from you, but they would even make it a higher price to pay whenever you discover it, anticipating that you would eventually acquiesce.

This is why it is essential to know that, anything that is easily accessible is questionable.

This is also why nowadays knowing the truth has become even more burdensome, because some people are too negligent to go out of their way to find it for themselves, so they would reconcile with whatever a stranger would teach them, as long as it sounds good and they do not have to do anything on their own.

Which is scored as another point for the opposing team.

Years ago, our parents taught us as children to never trust a stranger, but yet, some people have become adults and somehow the words of the wise are long forgotten.

Now we could easily point the blame toward the foreigners for indulging this ball of confusion concerning our identities upon our people, but we must also point the blame toward our very own people for not taking the responsibility of ameliorating the problem by now.

I mean think about it, the only real

reason why people even know about the story of their ancestors being allegedly captured somehow from Africa, by a few pale faces that traveled by way of a sailboat to whatever parts of Africa you choose, during a said time of no wars occurring in Africa, and then being forcefully brought to America, to slave for them or rather work for them, was because a stranger taught them that in school.

People failed to question their teachers, as to where they got this information from. People do not know the authors of American history personally, so that means that they never met a day in their life.

People will not bother with checking

the records of primary sources, where strangers claim they retrieved all of this information from, and then the so-called African-Americans can't even pick up the phone and call one of their direct living relatives that currently resides in any parts of the Africa continent right now, but those that can successfully conduct this task are not referred to as "African-Americans" today.

That is a big problem if I do say so myself because this reveals that the stories concerning antebellum America were purposely taught incorrectly throughout compulsory educational history curriculums.

Wasn't America's so-called slavery

abolished in 1865?

Because, then that means your grandmother's mother would have passed down the stories of slavery from her mother's mother, to your grandmother, then to your mother, and then down to you right?

As of today, the year 1865 is only one hundred and fifty-seven years ago, and that's not a long time to the point where you can not check and see for yourself what happened with your family individually.

Check and see if your direct ancestors were sold on some auction block like the foreign writers of American history would claim.

Check and see if your ancestors' names

are on those index passenger lists of those so-called slave ships that arrived on American soil from Africa. It's not impossible to know the truth because those records exist still today.

Can you recall any other group of people, no matter their skin complexion, being labeled primarily as the name of two continents? Not two countries, two continents.

That is known as a misnomer, which is "the act of applying a wrong name to some person or thing", and that should also be a major red flag to you.

Can you recall the reason why our people want to be referred to as a color, black, and then allow strangers to refer to them as black when realistically our skin complexions are different shades of the color brown?

This means that there is no such thing as black people and it only exists by the use of people's imagination being malevolently influenced yet again by a stranger's manipulative indoctrination.

Previously, the word black was used in a derogatory sense towards the Niiji up until the 1960s when some mysterious manipulation occurred abruptly, and our very own people, as young adults and especially college students, began to claim that they were black and proud as a newly formed political trend beginning in 1964, but before that, we were lawfully labeled as

Indian, Negro, Mulatto, and then Colored by the U.S. government.

The etymology of the word "Black/Blac" means "colorless, or the absence of color", and we know this to be true because if you would turn off the electricity in your house during the late evening hours, you would only see darkness.

So, if we were just being lawfully labeled as colored previously, and now we are somehow consenting to be labeled as black, which is the absence of color, then we are inadvertently placing ourselves in a state of not being present as a group of people, non-existent, when it comes to our actual identities, and more importantly, when it comes to the law concerning our constant demands for justice from this government.

This stems directly from the spells of the English language, nearly every word that is associated with the term black was used in a negative sense, meaning that it has a negative connotation within its descriptive usage when referring to a group of people. In other words, it is an obstructive affirmation.

For example, when people say things like they are black and proud, they are inadvertently claiming that they do not exist and are proud of it. When people chant black power, they are promoting a promising campaign that leads to nowhere because it was not there, to begin with.

When people say "that is black excellence", they are visualizing a delusional superiority in hopes of conclusive recognition when in reality it does not exist.

Once people begin to think for themselves again, then they will ask the right questions, like: Should we continue to call ourselves black and uphold this ball of confusion when it comes to our true identities?

Should we continue to allow some strangers to slap us in the face, by labeling us whatever they want to call us, teaching us whatever they want to tell us, or even treating us however they want to treat us?

We have tons of reconstructing to do amongst ourselves beautiful people, and so before we start to care about other places and other people again, let's be sure that we take care of home first this time because our ancestors made some mistakes that allowed for these foreign tenants to become our landlords, but the good thing about mistakes is that you learn from them, so you won't ever make that same mistake twice.

Chapter One

The Introduction Of The Gospel

Many absurd theories were deemed as official accounts of American history beginning in the 16th-Century, which is the calendar years between 1500 and 1599. Often regarded as the High Renaissance era, the 16th-Century saw vast unprecedented changes throughout the world, and especially in England, once trade and industry became trending courses of action.

With the help of prominent denominations of Christianity, Protestantism rose to the top of importance once the previous Renaissance era began to shift its focus on spreading the gospel to foreign parts during the age of discovery.

The gospel not only included Roman Catholic Christianity as a religious tradition that forced non-believers to become newly indoctrinated worshipers without choice, but it also included the introduction of newly established branches of science, like anthropology and psychology.

This granted prominent colonial rulers, scholars, and scientists to be racially biased in their approach to teaching many forms of science, politics, and orthodox religion. It also persuaded public perception of how they should conduct their everyday lives.

For example, Pope Gregory XIII, born Ugo Boncompagni, was the head of the

Catholic Church, and he was also the ruler of the Papal States from 1572 until his death in 1585.

It was said that he instituted the Gregorian Calendar in 1582, and this chart of time is currently still in use today, especially in landmasses colonized and governed by the many Christianity societies that still exist as well.

Religion was a utilitarian tool when it came to colonization, especially in America. For example, in 1701, a congregation was established in order to send ordained Christian missionaries out to the New World, to teach this gospel and hand out Bibles and prayer books to the indigenous people of America.

Hoping that this would soon allow the Indians to become weak and submissive by voluntarily converting to foreign religious practices and beliefs. Primarily to quell any possible Indian wars that could arise, and also to allow for the great migration of Eurasians to be welcomed as new native Americans as soon as possible.

It was initially called The Congregation For Propagating The Gospel In Foreign Parts, but the society's name was changed numerous times over the years to prevent any legal retaliation from those who were affected by their malicious actions in the name of God.

This was not the first nor the last religious society established with similar orders from the Virginia Company of London, nor was America the only target of colonization but parts of the West Indies were included as well.

Beginning in April of 1606, King James I of England chartered the Virginia Company, which was a commercial trading company, with orders to colonize the eastern coast of North America, dispatching over one-hundred Christian missionaries to America between present-day North Carolina and New York in December of 1606.

The Indians retaliated every instance a foreigner was spotted, making it more difficult for the incoming foreigners to run away from their slave masters in Eurasia, however, some Indians were able to be penetrated and indoctrinated.

Like the Lenape for example, a New Jersey indigenous tribe, in which the Scottish and the English immigrants utilized their waterways (like the Passaic, Musconetcong, Assunpink, Manasquan, Cohansey, Raritan, Crosswicks, Rancocas, Metedeconk, and the Topanemus) as guides for settlement patterns of migrating to American shores.

The Lenape assisted British proprietors by allowing them to purchase tracts of land along the Topanemus Brook in Monmouth County of East New Jersey in 1686.

According to the East New Jersey land deed -

"Pawmetop, Ishevekak, Neskorhock, Pamehelett, Indian owners and Sachems, to the Proprietors for a tract, beginning 1 1/2 mile from Amboy Bay near the path along the head of Cheesquakes, thence N. W. to the cove of Raraton River, along said river to the Round about, along the South R. to the Indian Fishingplace and to the Indian town Toponemes, thence to Hopp

River and along Jona than Holmes and John Bowne to the head of Chinquerorus."

A house of worship was established as the immigrant's main religious attraction in Topanemus, by Christian missionaries and a former Quaker preacher named George Keith, who was a Scottish-born land surveyor assigned the duty of East New Jersey, under the direction of the Society For Propagating The Gospel In Foreign Parts and the Church of England.

Chapter Two

The Starving Time

Through compulsory schooling beginning in the early 1900s, Americans were taught the gruesome fairytales of antebellum America, and how so-called black people were enslaved and forced to labor for majority-white slave masters.

The Niiji students of these schools were also taught that they are the descendants of these slaves that were somehow captured from parts of Africa and brought to North America on "slave ships".

However, it is essential to note that these parts of Africa, or rather countries in

Africa, were never authentically disclosed as official accounts of public records, nor does any country in Africa hold records of documentation of any slave trading transactions being conducted between themselves and colonizers residing in America at that time.

Being an African prisoner of an African-American war would be inaccurate because there were no wars between Africa and America during the so-called Transatlantic slave trade that can be validated.

Of course, being enslaved in Africa meant punishment for a crime conducted by that individual, but it means the same thing when it comes to being enslaved in England, France, Germany, and many other countries of Eurasia.

For example, between the 1700s and the 1900s, criminals or peasants throughout these parts of the world were enslaved, and as a punishment for their crimes, they were expelled from their countries of origin and transported to different countries on other continents as indentured servants or laborers.

This also reveals why the U.S. Census utilized the titles "Free Whites" and "Free Whites under 16 years of age" and then "Slaves" as the only classifications of status for particular people residing in America in 1790, and not because of their race or skin complexions categorically.

One-hundred and seventy-one years

prior to the establishment of the U.S. Census, the Virginia Company of London, under orders from King James I of England, was in the middle of attempting to settle in lands occupied by the Powhatan Indians near the Powhatan River (now called James River after King James) in 1619.

Even though writers of American history claim that the Virginia Company of London established settlements in the Powhatan territories in 1607, what they failed to mention is how the Powhatan Confederacy delivered resistance by raiding each new wave of intruding foreigners by orders from Chief Wahunsenacawh, the leader of the Powhatan Indians.

So the colony of Virginia was not

successfully established in 1607, due to the majority of the initial settlers being murdered before they could even disembark from their three sailboats; the Susan Constant, the Godspeed, and the Discovery, accompanied by captains Bartholomew Gosnold, Christopher Newport, and John Smith.

Watching his forty-man crew lose to the raiding Powhatans rapidly, captain John Smith was later captured while attempting to retreat by Powhatan Chief Opechancanough, who is prime Powhatan Chief Wahunsenacawh's younger brother.

Those that were able to retreat, like captain Christopher Newport, sent reports back to England concerning their encounters with the Algonquian-speaking Indians, and the Virginia Company quickly improvised their approach by including young boys with them on their next voyages to create a settlement in Powhatan territories in 1608.

This was done especially to make the Powhatan Indians feel guilt for murdering children as they raided. This plan later worked for a short period under strict conditions, due to the female Indians, who were mothers of their own children, feeling guilty about allowing the murder of other innocent children to take place.

In the latter part of 1609, the Englishmen and young boys that the Powhatan Indians eventually allowed to settle were met with another great crisis, as they were running extremely low on food and supplies and were too afraid to ask the Indians for assistance due to the possibility of being murdered.

According to one of the last survivors of 1609 that documented the direct accounts of the Jamestowne settlement, William Strachey, this was known as the "Starvation Period" or the "Starving Time" as these foreigners began to break and do the unthinkable for survival.

They had no choice but to eat random pieces of their clothing, like leather belts, cotton pants, straw hats, and wet shoes. Animals came dime a dozen during the winter drought, so they had no choice but to eat each other literally as they died from hypothermia, starvation, and disease. These conditions continued into 1610 and 1611.

During the warmer months of 1611, new arriving Englishman and young boys, governed by Lord Delaware, decided to remove themselves and the "Starving Time" survivors from the nearby Powhatan River and establish a new settlement 60 miles away.

Originally dubbed James Cittie by the English foreigners, named after King James I of England, they managed to survive the warmer months but were nearly on the brink of falling yet again during the winter months and into the next year.

The Starving Time

Between 1611 and 1612, the Virginia Company of London chartered more voyages that sent new settlers to James Cittie, in hopes that a permanent colony can finally be established with fewer complications and deaths by having more supplies and food to survive.

To take care of those in need, medics were also ordered onboard these voyages and one of these medics went by the name of John Rolfe.

Noticing the already established and active trade between the West Indians of the Caribbean Islands and the East Indians of Turtle Island, the English settlers made numerous attempts to get involved in the profitable enterprise, assuming that this could eventually allow them to become politically powerful.

They were unsuccessful in trading sassafras, lumber, silk and glass-made items, but John Rolfe allegedly learned how to grow another strain of tobacco from seeds that he allegedly obtained from the Caribbeans somehow.

This particular part of John Rolfe's story can not be validated by primary sources but this is what the writers of American history claim in order to give credit to John Rolfe for single-handedly developing the colony's first official profitable enterprise in Virginia in 1612.

It was also said that in 1614 John Rolfe married Pocahontas, who is Chief

Wahunsenacawh's daughter, which led to peace between the Powhatan Indians and the English foreigners, and then the Indians decided to convert to Christianity, but that is only true based on who you may ask.

Chapter Three

20 And Odd Negras

The Portuguese Empire's plan was set to establish forts on the continent of Africa by way of orders from King Phillip II of Spain. On February 11th, 1575, Paulo Dias de Novias, a Spanish captain-governer, explored west-central Africa scouting for indeterminate lands to select as their first official European city in Africa.

The first colony was established when Paulo Dias founded

Sao Paulo de Luanda, near the island of Luanda, which became the capital of then Portuguese Angola.

The Portuguese waged war against all surrounding territories like the Kingdom of Ndongo and the Kingdom of Kongo, just to name a few, murdering more African men and women than capturing and deporting them.

The captives that were deported were to be transported out of Africa to be used as laborers for the Spanish/Portuguese government, throughout their colonized possessions of lands referred to as New Spain.

During this time, New Spain consisted of territories of modern-day Mexico,

Central America, and nearly all of modern-day United States, and this also included the islands of the Caribbean, which was referred to as the Spanish West Indies.

This did not prevent other European powers, like England, the Netherlands, and France from claiming territories over landmasses Spain claimed for themselves.

The Portuguese realized that the trade of slaves was big business but they were limited due to having smaller sailboats within their fleets, raising the difficulty higher each time an order was given to export their cargo and slaves from Africa to New Spain. With maximum capacities of seven to ten people for each sailboat, wherries, or skiffs utilized, they needed a better way to accomplish their missions.

In the spring days of April, in the year 1618, a Japanese-built Western Barbarian-style sailing ship arrived in the Philippines, with a maximum carrying capacity of approximately one hundred and eighty people, weighing nearly five hundred tons and armed with a total of sixteen cannons. The Portuguese dubbed this ship the San Juan Bautista, but if translated into English, it was called Saint John the Baptist.

After a few reminiscing descriptive conversations about the ship, and having worked with the Japanese on many occasions previously, it was then quickly sold to the Spanish government by the

Japanese the same day it arrived in the Philippines.

The Spanish government stated that the ship was purchased for the adamant purposes of carrying human cargo, and miscellaneous goods, and also to provide better defense mechanisms against their Dutch enemies.

In August of 1619, the San Juan Bautista was loaded with food, cargo, silver, and some gold, and they got as close as they could get to their maximum capacity of one hundred and eighty people on board, including young enslaved African females from Angola.

They were bound for Vera Cruz, located on the east coast of modern-day Mexico.

But when they reached the Gulf of Mexico, they were intercepted and attacked by two unidentified privateer vessels, according to records held by the National Archives of Spain.

These privateer vessels, or rather called pirate ships today, were ordered to take on similar missions of piracy while raiding territories along the Caribbeans, attacking and robbing any boats whom they thought were carrying silver and gold.

In this particular incident, the pirates found more than what they expected. Not only did they steal the silver and gold, but each captain of the British vessels also robbed the San Juan Bautista of a combined total of forty-four young female

Angola slaves, one ship carried twenty-one while the other carried twenty-three.

Each ship headed to the West Indies in hopes to trade these slaves for goods. Having to report all transactions back to the Virginia Company of London, John Rofle documented in his journal that each of these ships arrived in Virginia days apart from each other.

He was very familiar with the second arriving ship, but he did not mention the name of the first arriving ship, indicating that he was unfamiliar with the unidentifiable ship.

Supporting a Dutch flag, this unidentified ship is called the White Lion, a British-built warship weighing one-hundred and fifty-six tons, not capable of carrying a large capacity of people like the much larger built Portuguese ship, San Juan Bautista. It can carry a maximum capacity of thirty people, and that's including cargo to last all people on board the ship for at least a week.

John Jope was the English captain of the White Lion, and this was his very first time sailing to the Virginia Colony. So he did not land in James Cittie, then referred to as Jamestowne at that time, as writers of American history claimed. He arrived in Point Comfort, Virginia, later known as Fort Monroe but now known as Hampton,

Virginia today.

Captain John Jope carried letters of marque with him. These were orders from the Dutch Prince Maurice of the Netherlands, granting him legal permission for his ship to sail as a privateer, and attack any Spanish or Portuguese ship it encountered.

John Jope unloaded the twenty-one Angola slaves in a rather coy demeanor, then people could not help but notice how bad of a condition they were in, making them not much of a great value to anyone who originally had any interest in hiring new indentured servants.

So in joint conjunction, both Governor Francis Wyatt and his "beloved friend"

Captain Willam Peirce, who was the Virginia Colony's cape merchant, traded supplies and food in exchange for two of the 20 and odd Negras, meaning dark-skinned females.

In John Rolfe's journal dedicated to Sir Edwin Sandys (spelled Edwyn Sandya by John) of the Virginia Company of London, in a broken Old-English way of speaking, John Rolfe wrote:

"About the latter end of August, a Dutch man of Warr of the burden of a 160 tunes arrived at Point-Comfort, the Commandors name Capt Jope, his pilot for the West Indies one Mr Marmaduke an Englishman. They met with the Trer in the West Indyes and dtermyned to hold consort shipp hitherward, but in their passage lost one the other. He brought not any thing but 20 and odd Negras, which the Governor and Cape Marchant bought for victualle at the best and easiest rate they could. He had a lardge and ample Comyssion from his Excellency to range and take purchase in the West Indyes."

The second British-built warship that arrived in Virginia only four days after the White Lion, did make its landing stop in

Jamestowne, Virginia in August of 1619. It was called the Treasuror, nearly identically built the same way as the White Lion, carrying twenty-three Angola servants, seven English settlers, cargo, food, and supplies that could last for one week.

These indentured servants were also in such bad shape that they were rejected by all interested parties involved. So the Treasuror then sailed to Bermuda to drop these servants off for possible provisions, and then returned to the Virginia Colony a few months later with West Indian servants onboard to also be traded for provisions.

According to John Roth's journal, the Treasuror had been in Jamestowne, Virginia many times before. Immigrating indigenous Niijis out of North America and out of the West Indies, and into Eurasia areas like England, France, Spain, and even the continent of Africa.

What is very important to note is how Virginia's Department of Historic Resources decided to alter John Rolfe's original quote to read as "20 and odd Negroes" in 1992, then it was changed again in 1994 to read as "20 and odd Africans", in order to suit the purpose of adding fictional accounts to the story.

For example, the VDHR indicated that captain John Jope carried both men and women indentured servants on board his ship, and a male and a female servant were traded with a plantation owner by the name of William Tucker of Point Comfort, Virginia for nothing more than food, however, there is no record of this transaction in existence.

Additional parts of this story were later added stating that the two Angola indentured servants that captain William Tucker received went by the names of Isabel and Anthony, which of course are not names in relation to the Bantu culture or language throughout Angola's region.

Then they went as far as to say that Isabel and Anthony mated and gave birth to the first official African American baby, naming the baby boy William Tucker after captain William Tucker, during the year 1624, however, none of this story can be validated by any publicly verifiable records which makes these people null and void, with exception of captain William Tucker but it is not crystal clear as to how and why he is called a captain, being as though no records exist of him owning a boat or enrolling to become a soldier of a military.

Another example of the VDHR adding fictional accounts to the story is the alteration of illustrated depictions that were originally utilized to tell this story from its existing primary sources.

The first official illustration in relation to this Jamestowne 1619 story was created on the date of January 2, 1754, which would be one hundred and thirty-five years after 1619. The original illustrator or artist of this depiction is not disclosed by the company that now owns this property, but as of today, it is #3190638 of the Hulton Archive collection owned by Getty Images and is being sold for $499 and up.

This image depicts Negra children, or dark-skinned female children, who are fully clothed and are not under any sort of threat, like being held at gunpoint for example. In fact, this image displays unarmed overseers or potential employers scouting to hire new able-body laborers.

It also depicts that the children have been, and are currently being, disembarked from a wherry or a skiff and not from a cargo ship or a "slave ship" as writers of American history would claim, being as though cargo ships were not commercially produced until the 1850s, nearing the tail end of slavery in America.

This particular depiction of the Jamestowne 1619 story was altered and reproduced, then later published by illustrator Howard Pyle for Harper's Weekly, Virginia's Department of Historic Resources (VDHR), and The Library of Virginia in 1917.

The description of Howard Pyle's version of this depiction reads: "Landing of Negroes at Jamestown from a Dutch Man-of-War 1619"

Howard Pyle's depiction included gaslighting accounts, that allowed the viewer of this image to believe that the new arriving servants were under threats of death, by depicting the employers or overseers, who have been changed around in this image, as now being armed and dangerous.

The children have been altered to be represented as teenage males, who were also not fully clothed and are being detained as if they were criminals.

Also, the skiff or wherry that they disembarked from is not present in this depiction, leaving the viewer to use their imagination, with supporting fictional storytelling of the 1900s, in order to believe the exaggerated and exacerbated versions of slavery in America by those who were selected to write about it.

Chapter Four

To Immigrate And To Emigrate (Prisoners of War)

It is essential to know the difference between the two words - immigrate and emigrate - because both words are pronounced the same but they initially do not carry the same meaning, especially during the time of what you are about to learn about throughout this book.

Webster's English Language Dictionary of 1828 defines the noun emigrant as "one who removes his habitation or quits one country or region to settle in another." While the noun immigrant is defined as "a person that removes into a country for the purpose of permanent residence".

Subscribing to the newly modified definitions of both words would allow readers to conclude that both words mean the same thing, however, readers who are familiar with the spells of the English language would know better than that.

Both words have common origins in Latin that separate the two words by definition. The Latin word "emigratus" means "to exit", and the Latin word "immigratus" means "to come into".

So an emigrant is an individual who moves from one region or a country, to live in another region but of that same country, and that is according to its etymology, which is "to remove from one state to another state or territory".

What is important to note here is that regions, states, and territories can be considered countries but not continents, so the meaning of immigrating is referring to a person or group of people that are removed from one continent to another.

The etymology of the word "immigrate" means " to pass into a place as a new inhabitant or resident, to move to a country where one is not a native, for the purposes of settling permanently there."

This does not sound peaceful at all where it says "for the purpose of settling permanently there", as a resident and not a native of that landmass.

This explains why the word "remove" was used in Webster's definitions of both words because wars were going on in America, and if a person became a slave following the aftermaths of these wars, then things were confiscated from that person, producing prisoners of war.

Chapter Five

Removing The Negro Population

In a letter to President Thomas Jefferson dated December 25th, 1810, John Lynch, who colonized lands he named after himself called Lynchburg, Virginia, made a descriptive proposition to Thomas Jefferson, that called for the "colonisation of the nigger people on the coast of affrica", so that a settlement can be established for immigrating the Niiji out of North America and into Africa somewhere along the coast, according to records held by the national archives.

John Lynch's letter was sponsored, inspired, and remotely authored by a woman named Anne Mifflin.

Anne Emlen Mifflin was a Quaker of the Evangelical Christian faith, she is also a descendant of European parents of the Reckless family that immigrated from what is known now as Combria, England, to North America during the late 1670s, at a time when Englishmen of the many denominations of the Christian faith, we're attempting to immigrate to North America, but could only sign land and peace treaties with a few of the prominent Indigenous elders, in which their tribes occupied the lands of West Jersey, Rhode Island, and Pennsylvania where Anne Mifflin was born and raised nearly 85 years later on April 20th, 1755.

According to lynch's letter to Thomas Jefferson, Anne Mifflin was a Quaker preacher that traveled to Lynchburg for an annual religious visitation to Virginia, where Quaker ministers from other States would hold formal meetings, but this time around, Anne and her fellow Quakers met with "a few noted characters" of Virginia to promote her new plan, that would not only quell the negro population and revolt issues quickly, but permanently, or so she thought at least.

In 1810 during September, Anne spoke with former Virginia governor, slaveholder, and General of the Militia named James Wood, who had just recently manumitted his indentured servants during this time. James Wood highly approved the plan and even offered to help promote it by endorsement.

Anne planned to target the freed negros

of the southern states and emigrate them all to an island called Bolama, on the coast of West Africa, in which the majority section of that landmass is now known today as Sierra Leone, but the only issue at that time that she noted, was that it was currently being colonized by the British government.

Also, Anne Mifflin immediately earned the support of Granville Sharp, an English abolitionist who campaigned throughout most of his adult life, during the 1760s, to end the Indian slave trade in both Europe and America.

Sharp was also an influential founding member, of the British lead "Society For The Abolition Of The Slave Trade", which was established in 1787, and the British colonial corporation called the "Sierra Leone Company" in 1792.

With a previous attempt to settle the issue of the multiple rebellions continuously occurring all across America during his presidency, Thomas Jefferson received this letter from John Lynch and eagerly responded a year later, on January 21st, 1811, by stating that this is "the most desirable measure which could be adopted for gradually drawing off the Negro population".

Stating more favorable opinions of the letter, he later added:

"Indeed, nothing is more to be wished than that the United States should themselves undertake to make such an establishment on the coast of Afrikka"

Having been the former third president of the United States of America, and succeeded by the current president at that time, James Madison Jr., Thomas Jefferson's statements on the proposition was well-received by nearly all colonisationalist in North America.

Chapter Six

Immigrating The Negro

Thomas Jefferson's statements influenced more politicians, and religious organizations, to form meetings to strengthen the cause for removing the indigenous Niiji, or as they loved to call our ancestors, the Negroes.

The Union Humane Society was founded in the year of 1815, in the State of Ohio, by Benjamin Lundy.

This organization was said to have been against slavery, however, writers of American history fail to mention the dark side of its racially motivated causes of action against the so-called Negroes.

First, the organization emphasized the necessity of "common action by all forces interested in the amelioration of the Negro race".

And then second, the organization recommended as a basis for common action - "the removal of the Negroes beyond the pale of the white man."

While the Union Humane Society failed to assist other States on a national scale basis, the Kentucky Colonization Society stepped in, with stronger terms to fill in the gaps.

According to the National Archives, the Kentucky Colonization Society took advantage of the close of the War of 1812, and the existence of the vast tracts of inappropriate lands in the United States.

The members of the organization immediately realized that the number of free Niiji were rapidly increasing daily, and that the government needed to act right now.

At its annual meeting that was held in Frankfort on October 18th and 19th in 1815, they noted that the territories open for Niiji to reside were greatly restricted, due to the "prohibitory legislation existing in many States".

So they petitioned Congress that a suitable territory would be -

"laid off as an asylum for all those niggers who have been, and those who may hereafter be, emancipated within the United States; and that such donations, allowances, encouragements, and assistance be afforded to them as necessary for carrying them thither and settling them therein; and that they be under such regulations and government in all respects as your wisdom shall direct."

This added more fuel to the already existing flame, but the government had trouble offering funds, and other governmental assistance, like a six-month repayment term set for the money-hungry local Afrikan leaders and officials of the poor colony of what is known now as Sierra Leone, during the years of 1816 and 1817, but, as long as they kept the "niggers that the United States will ship in."

Chapter Seven

The Establishment Of The American Society For Colonizing The Free People Of Color In The United States Of America

This trouble that was just mentioned arose when the British government received a notice of what the United States government was attempting to do, to a colony that they owned. So the US government did not budge until the very next year, with a slightly different plan.

During the year 1816, a racist bigoted politician and slaveholder or employer rather, by the name of Charles Fenton Mercer, whose parents immigrated from

England to North America during the early 1700s, grew more fearful and angry towards the government's progress in removing the Niiji from North America to a distant territory.

So in the Spring of the year 1816, Mercer somehow discovered the secret action of the Virginia Assembly, soon after one of the "negro insurrections" took place very near his residence of Fredericksburg, Virginia that same year.

He overheard that there were two resolutions directing the governor of Virginia, by the name James Barbour, to correspond with the president of the United States at that time, who was James Madison Jr., to secure lands somewhere that will act as a territory suited for colonization of emancipated laborers or rather freed indentured servants.

Mercer accidentally came at the very end of the session for him to present his manipulative program to the assembly, so he waited for the next session to take place.

In the meantime, Mercer broke the bar of secrecy and conducted business interviews with a few of the Virginia Assembly members. Those members were Francis S. Key of Georgetown and Elijah B. Caldwell of the City of Washington, and with their advice drew some rather malevolent but distinguished propositions of resolutions, that they eventually introduced to the

Virginia Assembly during its next session.

Their resolutions called for the:

"National government to find a territory on the North Pacific on which to settle free niggers and nigger mulattos those afterwards emancipated in Virginia."

These resolutions have since been changed by the Senate to read as:

"On the North Pacific or the African coast."

And it was passed by the Virginia Assembly on December 21st, 1816.

On the same day of its passing by Virginia, when asked to present a statement on why he supports his resolutions before reading them to the president, and many other political powers involved, Mercer stated:

"Many thousands of the white individuals in our native State, as you well know Mr. President, are restrained from manumitting their slaves, as you and I are, by the melancholy conviction that they can not yield to the suggestions of humanity without manifesting injury to their country."

Mercer adamantly reminded the public, that the rapidly increasing free Niiji population was allegedly "endangering the peace of the States and impaired, in a large section, the value of slave property", calling them "vicious free niggers".

Mercer stated:

"Vicious free niggers, sally forth from their coverts, beneath the obscurity of night, and plunder the rich proprietors of the valleys. They infest the suburbs of the towns and cities, where they become the depositories of stolen goods, and, schooled by necessity, elude the vigilance of our defective police."

This very first public meeting which consisted of many European immigrants who were racist colonizationalists and politicians, was held in the City of Washington, now known as Washington, D.C., on the same day of December 21st, 1816, and from this very meeting, the American Society For Colonizing The Free People Of Color In The United States Of America, now known as the American

Colonization Society, was established.

Mercer's resolutions were passed by the House, seven days before this meeting took place, on December 14th, 1816, and the Senate passed it soon after this meeting was adjourned on December 21st, 1816.

According to the 4th Annual Report of the American Society For Colonizing The Free People Of Color In The United States Of America, which was started by the Kentucky Colonization Society that I mentioned earlier, the organization dispatched a representative on December 25th, 1821 named Dr. Eli Ayres to "purchase land farther north of the coast from Sierra Leone".

Accompanied by US Naval forces with

Captain Stockton, they held the leaders of the aboriginal African tribes of Baza and Dey by gunpoint, demanding that they take the short deal that the US government is offering them, in trade for their land then called Montserado but now known as Cape Mesurado, or die.

By forcefully purchasing the land of Cape Mesurado for alleged trade goods, weapons, rum, and other supplies worth a total equivalent to just three hundred dollars, the Republic of Liberia was established in the year 1821, and thousands of Niiji, who are indigenous to the lands of North America, were forcefully immigrated to the coast of what is known now as West Africa, for the very first time during the history of the existence of the

United States, and the city of Monrovia was established the very next year, on the date of April 25th, 1822.

This is just one of the many reasons why the so-called Transatlantic slave trade story was told to us all in reverse.

Chapter Eight

The Correlation Between Africans And American Indians

Recent reports that surfaced around the internet indicate that Southern African natives feel threatened by their very own people, and are resulting in the use of deadly force to send a message to other incoming South African foreigners who are in transient status to their motherland.

These reports are calling this uprising of native South African attacks, Xenophobia, which is defined as "the fear of strangers or a hatred of foreigners, or anything that is strange or foreign."

But how can this be, when in the minds

of most Americans, people from Africa are all one people. So how could one African consider another African to be a foreigner?

Let's break this down a little more.

The term Xenophobia was created from two separate words, Xenos and "phobia". Phobia is defined as the "fear of strangers", or so one may think.

The term Xenos is derived from the Greek word Xenia, which means "guest-friendship". Now in Greek

Mythology, it was prudent for an individual to extend hospitality to a stranger (Xenos) because it was not known if the stranger was a god or a goddess.

This means that the word "phobia" was

used to imply that a stranger, that could be a friend, is being feared or now hated.

What is also very important to note, is that the 1884 etymology of the word Xenophobia meant Agoraphobia, which is "a fear of places and situations that might cause panic, helplessness, or embarrassment. An anxiety disorder caused by panic attacks."

This is to imply that if a person did not fully accept a stranger with kindness and hospitality while unknowing that stranger's true motives, that person would somehow appear to be crazy, and could possibly have panic attacks.

This brings us to the recent Xenophobic attacks in South Africa, which are just now surfacing heavily everywhere on social media, but Google reports that these attacks were made known to the public in May 2008, which is well over a decade ago, so why are we just hearing about them now?

Especially since South Africans have been fighting against foreigners and strangers that were invading their lands, from doing business on their lands, and from foreigners that were trying to govern them on their lands, since the early 1800s to be quite frank. This should all ring a bell here.

Chapter Nine

The Indians Are The Niiji

Now before we go any further, I want you to make note of the noun Indian and how this term was defined by author Noah Webster of the Webster's English Language Dictionary of the year 1828.

Webster defined the noun "Indian" in the year 1828 as "a general name of any native of the Indies; as an East Indian or West Indian, it is particularly applied to any native of the American continent."

So, when you hear me use the term Indian to refer to the indigenous people of the American continent, note that I am not referring to the people of the landmass now known as India, as of January 25th, 1950, which was originally known as "Indostan" and its most Northern region called "Hindustan", before the establishment of the Republic of India in the 1950s.

This particular landmass of India was never called India before the early 1900s. The people of the landmass now known as India would still refer to their motherland as Barhat or Indostan today.

You may recall hearing that the term "Nigger" was used by those who fell victim to preconceived notions or prejudice within their families, that can only be taught to an individual at a young age, exposing just how vulnerable their families truly are, by allowing strangers to manipulate their minds with a set of beliefs that have never been proven or even questioned for that matter.

The term "Nigger" should not be used as a means to call upon each other in a positive sense, especially when it originated from a word that was used in a negative sense, deriving from the word "niggard" which means "an extremely stingy person", but then over the years, we somehow allowed it to be adopted still.

Also, our people were historically called Indians, but not by each other during the earliest days of American colonization, only by foreigners from another continent that did not have our people's best interest whatsoever, but we eventually allowed it to be adopted still.

You may recall me using the term Niiji when referring to the indigenous people of America, along with their descendants, because Niiji is an ancient descriptive term that defines all aboriginal people that have indigenously inhabited the landmass historically called Turtle Island.

Turtle Island refers only to particular western areas of the supercontinent known as Gondwana, which includes Canada, North, Central, and South America, along with the surrounding Pacific Islands. These landmasses are commonly referred to as Turtle Island for many heavily spiritually inclined reasons.

The simplest reason is due to its shape depicted on various maps of West Gondwana, as though all of the edges of the landmass visually form the shape of a prehistoric turtle. But then it goes a lot deeper than just some random illusion and a so-called myth.

The first is the turtle's historic background, in which the legacy of the turtle stretches far beyond what the Gregorian calendar can detect.

Terrestrial Turtles have been alive before anything was ever written down, pre-dating western colonialism and western civilization, and even the births of all foreign oral gospels. So the turtle has been there, done that, lasting even beyond what is known as the Jurassic era.

They live on land and are ones with nature, and just those few things alone represent a mutual spiritual connection between the turtle and the indigenous Niiji. Parts of Turtle Island are viewed as the shell of a great turtle.

The shell of the turtle is structured by about 60 or more of its bones, and it can not be easily penetrated by an invading predator. This also represents the ancestral spirits of indigenous Niiji. We are warriors, and during times of war, our ancestors did not take it easy on foreign invaders.

For centuries and centuries, our ancestors revolted against invading enemies, and once the strongest Chiefs of many of the largest families were lost at war, then and only then the shell was fractured, but that is not a permanent misfortune, because a turtle can actually heal itself from a fractured shell and recover from its injuries, and so can you.

The term Niiji was directly used as a positive means to refer to an ally or an associate by numerous indigenous families throughout the Americas and Canada, however, the term Niiji should not be confused with the word "friend".

You will hear the word "friend" being commonly used nowadays by every American, but, have you ever thought about its initial usage or even its original definition before?

Its recorded origin derives from the mid-1600s and is used in one of the most popularized pidgin languages of that time period, English, which was later known as Old English. The word "friend" was originally defined as "a Quaker", or "a member of the Religious Society of Friends", and also during this time period, the antonym of the word friend is "fiend", which basically drops the letter "r" in the word friend, and it was defined as "an enemy".

Nowadays the word "fiend" is used to describe a person that has an overwhelming substantial amount of interest in something, whether it's good or bad, but originally the Quakers referred to each other as "friend" and referred to any other groups of people as "fiend" which describes their enemies, evil spirits or the devil.

Since our ancestors were not Quakers at that time nor were they members of the Religious Society of Friends, then it's quite obvious who they were referring to when using the word "fiend", and this is why "friend" and "Niiji" have no correlations.

The origins of the term Niiji derives from the indigenous Algonquin language, which was a language spoken in multiple different dialects or accents by various families throughout the Americas, and even parts of Canada over time.

After the indigenous Niiji of America was infiltrated by the foreign influence that led to many deadly wars, mainly against our very own people due to their betrayals, the Algonquin language became one of the few languages adopted by extended families that found themselves chiefless after the wars subsided.

Niiji was used to describe an ally and was traditionally used amongst indigenous men towards each other, and prior to this word being adopted by many, it was chiefly used by the Anicinape family as the short version of their Ojibwe/Algonquin-based word, called "Niijikiwenh" which means "my brother".

And according to the Department of American Indian Studies of Minnesota, the word Niiji is defined in English as "my brother, my cousin, or my fellow man", and throughout the years of American colonization, Niijis were fictitiously labeled as various misnomers and derogatory social constructs; such as "people of color", "coloureds", "negroes", "mulattos", "creoles", "niggers", "blacks", and now "African-American"; all given to us by only foreign squatters migrating from other countries of the surrounding continents to keep us all separated.

So when you hear me use the word Niiji, now you know that I am strictly referring to my extended family throughout the Americas, or Turtle Island, with the utmost respect for who they truly are and what our ancestors fought and died for.

Chapter Ten

The Agenda Of The American Colonization Society

The rioting and insurrections occurring throughout South Africa were very similar to the Indian riots and insurrections that took place in America.

This is also why the American Colonization Society was created in order to carry out the political and religious plan of shipping, or immigrating, the indigenous Niiji of America, to near vacant lands along the coast of Africa during the late 1800s.

This was never about some so-called slaveholders setting their slaves free, this was about people that had a slaveholder mentality but were afraid of the indigenous people that chose not to be slaves to strangers.

A fear existed that the Niiji would one day rise from being prisoners of war, because, whereas many of the Indian tribes immediately killed foreigners for encroaching upon their lands, there were those indigenous people that instead bestowed friendship and hospitality towards the incoming strangers.

Some of the Niiji began to do business with these strangers and even worked alongside them, while in other cases, the newly settled strangers were under the premise that they would be paid according to the work conducted; like farming, expanding the railroad, or even building towns, etc.

These particular indigenous people were the traders and also considered traitors of their own kind, and to the incoming strangers, those that accepted them were regarded as friends of the Indians.

So in other words, when strangers are being accepted by Indian traitors, then they can easily portray themselves as friends to the indians, which will further allow them to hide any malevolent intent, while also providing the strangers a route to become closer than what other strangers may be allowed to do so by non-friendly Indians.

Because, if you may recall what was

mentioned earlier, the definition of the term "friend" is a Quaker of the Christian faith, this means that if you are regarded as a friend to the Indians, then you are now one who is accepted to preach the gospel of Christianity to the Indians.

So as more of the pale-faced foreigners immigrated to America, more Indian lands were being confiscated through the process of land-grabbing. The term land-grab is defined as a usually swift acquisition of property (such as land or patent rights) often by fraud or force.

These motions caused a rift amongst the indigenous people of this land, setting tribes against other tribes, especially for those indigenous people who were against new customs, new religions, new governments, and even the expansion of foreigners being thrust upon them as new residents.

Chapter Eleven

Paper Genocide

There were several Indian Wars between the late 1700s and the early 1800s. These wars were amongst the tribes themselves and also against incoming immigrants from foreign countries of other continents.

These wars were also regarded as "Indian raids, Indian campaigns, Indian riots, Indian revolts, Indian rebellions, and Indian ambushes", which were to keep the settlers or strangers from encroaching west of the Appalachian mountains.

King George III's Proclamation of 1763 was a plea bargain to the current

Governors, multiple governments, and also the Commanders in Chiefs of the colonies of America, asking them not to cross further into any non-friendly Indian territories, due to the continuous loss of their comrades that were brutally murdered during the wars with the Indians of America.

These European settlers or strangers during this time previously derived from the very tiny provinces of Britannia, or Britannica, which was originally known as the Island of Albion but is now known today as Great Britain.

And according to this Proclamation of 1763, they all joined forces with the governments controlling the landmass known as Hispania, which is known today as Spain, and the landmass called Gaul, which is now known today as France.

This is when Britannia and their new allies, became "Great" through the "advice of our said Privy council, granted Our Letters Patent under Our Great Seal of Great Britain", meaning that all said governments are now under the full control of the Crown, or corporation, now known as Great Britain.

This same Proclamation of 1763 gave mention to the "Definitive Treaty of Peace, concluded at Paris the Tenth Day of February" of that same year. This means that there was a Treaty of Paris in 1763, before the Treaty of Paris of 1783, that is so duly noted by those self-proclaimed history buffs today.

The initial Treaty of Paris was created in 1763 to pretend as if they were governmentally separating from each other, stating -

"In order to re -establish peace on solid and durable foundations, and to remove forever all subject of dispute with regard to the limits of the British and French territories on the continent of America; it is agreed, that, for the future, the confines between the dominions of his Britannick Majesty and those of his Most Christian Majesty, in that part of the world, shall be fixed irrevocably by a line drawn along the middle of the River Mississippi."

This allowed France to possess one side of the territory of America while Britain possesses the other, but still left room for Spain to control some of this territory as well, while all of America was currently occupied by the Indians simultaneously, being as though they were the original inhabitants of America, to begin with.

Additionally, one of the main reasons why the first Treaty of Paris of 1763 was established was to initiate the so-called "American Revolution" by creating conflicts between the indigenous peoples themselves.

The 15th-century definition of "revolution" places it as a great change in affairs, calling it "an overthrow of an established political system".

So the foreigners of the thirteen colonies, who were still under the British Crown even after forming the United States of America in 1776, birthed a new alliance between themselves and the Indians once trade became a viral trend.

The French and the British followed suit with this new alliance as well making trade between themselves and the Indians a reality.

This created much confusion and fighting amongst the tribes on American soil because they were forced to choose a side. This resulted in many Indigenous chiefs being killed off, and with that, came a reconstruction era within the tribes.

The American Revolution, commonly known as the American Revolutionary War, ended once Britain signed the Definitive Treaty of Peace and Friendship between his Britannick Majesty and the United States of America on September 3rd, 1783, which provided for "the restitution of all estates, rights, and properties which have been confiscated belonging to real British subjects."

It is also important to note that this Treaty was originally introduced as a preliminary treaty, known as the Provisional Treaty with France and Spain, which was introduced on November 30th, 1782.

Then seven years later, the United

States of America began operating under a new Constitution on March 9th, 1789, which was created to establish a uniform rule of Naturalization, laws regarding congress, currency, taxation, and rules for the government and regulation of land, as the United States.

Now keep in mind that this was after agreements were previously signed between Britain, France, and Spain.

So by having this constitution set in place, which was secretly created to replace the Articles of Confederation, many of the American Indian tribes continued to welcome these foreign immigrants to America unmolested, due to being under the guise of Xenos, baring the slight possibility of some formal faith in their "guest-friendship" undivulged.

Chapter Twelve

The Indian Wars That Led To White Tears

The foreign residents or squatters of transient status were later allowed to become naturalized citizens of the thirteen colonies, however, it was still under the rule of the British Crown. Article 1 - Section 2 of the United States Constitution gave congressional seats based solely on the population count of America at that time:

"Representatives and direct taxes shall be apportioned among the several states which may be included within this Union, according to their respective numbers, which shall be determined by adding to the whole number of free Persons, including those bound to service for a term of years, and excluding Indians not taxed, three-fifths of all other Persons."

So the very next year, the initial U.S. Census was established on what was known as "Census Day" on August 2nd, 1790.

Foreigners were then able to see how many people of color were actually within many of the tribes on this land. And this was a noticeable increase in population from what they originally expected.

It is also important to note that the majority of these people of color were free men, women, and children and not your commonly known depictions of so-called slaves.

Only 32% of the population of Virginia were allegedly slaves during the early 1800s, but keep in mind, during this time, Virginia also included areas that later became the States of Kentucky, West Virginia, and Maryland, along with other lands of the Southwest Territory.

According to the U.S. Census Bureau, thousands of census records have either been removed or destroyed, due to either water, smoke, or fire damage, affecting most census records ranging from the 1790 census up to the 1930 census.

And when it comes to Virginia, the U.S. Census stated -

"As the federal census schedules of

the state of Virginia for 1790 are missing, the list of the state enumerations made in 1792, 1783, 1784, and 1785 have been substituted, and while not complete, they will undoubtedly prove of great value."

In the early 1800s, the pale-faced enumerators of the U.S. Census Bureau, and even the small variants of marshals and sheriffs of particular counties and regions of the South, grew more fearful of the ever-growing population of the Indians, now called Negroes or Coloureds or People of Color during this time.

Most enumerators refused to travel the lands that mainly Indians occupied, due to the threat of being murdered intensified rapidly by ongoing riots, rebellions, revolts, and insurrections occurring across America, causing the majority of the final population count for the Indians, or rather the "free people of color" as the U.S. Census claims, to be royally unsubstantiated and inaccurate.

Not only that, the reports of much larger populations of Indians that occupied all the rest of America, that were not recorded by the Census due to not being settled by any foreign person, toppled the governments of said surrounding states, which caused, even more, fear and panic amongst the pale-faced foreigners knowing that their population in America was realistically much smaller.

As more of the Indians became

cognizant of the government's broken promises, treaties, bad business deals, and betrayals of foreign trade, the wars continued, and so did the pace of brutal violence.

Now simultaneously, Indians that occupied the lands now known as Haiti today, were also under attack from the newly formed France, Spain, and Britain trinity, beginning in 1791, and finally ending twelve years later, by "defeating the French Commander and a large part of his Army, in November 1803 the viscount de Rochambeau surrendered the remnant of the expedition", then Haiti declared its independence on January 1st, 1804.

But, just before this war ended, which

was known as the Haitian Revolution, a very notable bill was passed in America, which allowed for the purchase of a large landmass known as the Louisiana Territory, which included states now known today as Arkansas, Missouri, Iowa, Oklahoma, Kansas, Nebraska, Minnesota, North Dakota, South Dakota, New Mexico, Texas, Montana, Wyoming, Colorado, and Louisiana, it also covered part of the Canadian Provinces, Alberta and Saskatchewan.

In Congressional records, this purchase was dubbed the Louisiana Purchase and the treaty was signed in Paris on April 30th, 1803, but it was not ratified until October 20th, 1803.

Chapter Thirteen

Sent To Africa, Not From Africa

So if Haiti was successful at winning the war against foreign immigrants, which they were, then what caused the Indians of America to lose against these same foreign immigrants?

The answer to this question is very simple: the illusion of inclusion.

In earlier chapters, we covered detailed information concerning the campaigns of particular missionaries who called for the removal of the so-called Negro population, referring to the Indians of course, due to the pale faces wanting more land to reside on, and to possibly quell the Indian wars that were continuously occurring against them.

So with the establishment of The American Society For Colonizing The Free People of Color In The United States Of America, which was later renamed, the American Colonization Society, what was done exactly for our people to agree with getting on a boat, and traveling to a distant location, unknowing of the perils that may lay ahead of them on some foreign territory?

Could it be that colonization had become glorified, to a point that some of the Indians just wanted to join the club?

What is Colonization?

It is "the act of colonizing, to establish

a colony, to migrate and settle in as inhabitants for the purpose of cultivation, commerce or defense, and for permanent residence."

So could it be possible that the indigenous Niiji that migrated to West Africa did so under a false pretense, and not because they were slaves and their slave masters set them free, but because they saw themselves as colonizers going to a foreign land to spread the gospel to those indigenous people in Africa?

The Indians that were chosen by churches to settle into Sierra Leone and Liberia for example were called newly found missionaries, a title given to those who abide by the church by spreading the gospel, which required a formal application, and those who were chosen were hand-selected to carry out this duty. This was a movement to teach "uncivilized persons" and natives how to worship the God of the Bible.

According to Annual Reports of the American Colonization Society -

"The Government has inaugurated treaties with many of the tribes, and a definite understanding and their good-will have been obtained. Calls are frequent from these people for instruction in divine truth and the useful arts, that the Christianizing and civilizing power of true religion and advanced industrial skill may be employed in the regeneration of that inviting region.

Numerous Aborigines, in order to secure the advantages of proximity to the civilized settlements, are flocking from the interior and building villages near the Liberians. Zodaque, a Pessah Chief, has lately arrived with some two hundred followers and is located near Crozerville. Another Chief, with about three hundred refugees from heathenism, is expected soon to settle in the same neighborhood."

Chapter Fourteen

Factors Of Expatriation

This is the real truth as to why the American Indians migrated to West Africa, because they saw themselves as colonizers, being as though they were enticed by the promises of the possibilities of having free land, free money, and a form of recognition, but what they did not see, was the bill that was proposed in front of Congress for Expatriation.

The Webster's English Language Dictionary of 1828 defines the word "expatriation" as "banishment". To expatriate means to "banish oneself, to quit one's country, with a renouncing citizenship and allegiance, to take residence and become a citizen in another country."

According to the Federal Judicial Center, Thomas Bolling Robertson was born on February 27, 1779, in Petersburg, Virginia. He was a Judge for the U.S. District Court for both the Eastern and Western Districts of Louisiana.

Thomas was also both the Governor and the Attorney General of Louisiana, and was even a member of the U.S. House of Representatives for Louisiana's at-large district, in which he introduced a bill for Expatriation during a Congressional session in February 1818, stating

- "...there is a consequence for allowing

naturalization." "...it is a clear principle, then, that every free man has the right to quit his country, whether his country by birth or adoption, and to live in some other, whether it be for the benefit of his health, or to procure the necessaries, conveniences, or luxuries of life, or because he may prefer the political institutions of some other country to those of his own, or for any other reason whatever."

So in other words, if immigrating foreigners were never allowed to naturalize here in the U.S. before the introduction of this Expatriation bill, then, they would not have the right to expatriate, because Naturalization is "the act of investing an alien with the rights and privileges of a native subject or citizen."

So under this bill, foreigners are then fraudulently allowed to lawfully remove the indigenous people from their homelands, legally.

During the year 1818, Congress did not have the constitutional right to pass this said bill, but Thomas was eager enough to point out the fact that State legislatures did. He used Virginia as an example, in which the "Virginia law" provided a way for expatriation to be legally exercised.

Speaking on this Virginia law, Thomas Robertson stated that -

"It provides that the citizen intending to expatriate himself, shall state the fact on the records of a court of the United States; and that on his departing and going out of the United States, he shall be considered as having exercised his right of expatriation. It is in substance, a copy of the Virginia Act."

This bill was introduced as a precursor to how a legal banishment may be able to take place, for those states wishing to remove their free "Negro populations".

The formation of colonization societies in each state was encouraged in Congress, and two years later, the first missionaries were sent by the American Colonization Society to West Africa.

So in conclusion, people of today's society in America have been misinterpreting and also misrepresenting what a fact actually means, due to what they have been indoctrinated and conditioned to believe how a fact is psychologically and socially determined.

For example, a person would normally consider traditional information given to them to be a fact without noticing that they just inadvertently allowed someone's opinion to be considered valuable as a source of credible information.

In other words, just because someone else states repetitive information, that you may have heard about before during let's say your school days or your teenage years, for example, does not necessarily mean that the information given is true.

If you should not judge a book by its cover, and your parents informed you as a child that you should never talk to strangers, then why would a person believe that someone's opinion is a fact when the people that gave you this information are total strangers, and you're allowing them to do your thinking for you?

#ImJustHereToMakeYouThink

It Was Told In Reverse

The Untold Truth About The Transatlantic Slave Trade

By Dane and Taneisha Calloway

Bibliography

"Instructions for the Virginia Colony 1606", George Welling, University of Groningen, 2012

"A Historical Account of the Incorporated Society for the Propagation of the Gospel in Foreign Parts", David Humphreys, London, 1718

"Sixty-Seventh Annual Report of the American Colonization Society, with the Minutes of the Annual Meeting and the Board of Directors", Washington City: Colonization Building, 450 Pennsylvabia Avenue, 1884

"The Statutes at Large; Being A Collection of all the Laws of Virginia, from the First Session of the Legislature, in the year 1619", Volume 1 - 13, William Waller

Hening, 1800 - 1823

"The Revised Code of the Laws of Virginia: Being A Collection of all such Acts of the General Assembly, of a Public and Permanent Nature, as are now in Force", Thomas Nitchie, Volume 1 - 13, 1800 - 1825

"Two broad-sides against tobacco the first given by King James of famous memory, his Counterblast to tobacco: the second transcribed out of that learned Physician Dr. Everard Maynwaringe, his treatise of the scurvy", Josuah Sylvester, 1672

"Causal Killing Law", Hening, Statutes, Volume II, 1669 Price, David A. "Love and Hate in Jamestown: John Smith,

Pocahontas, and the Start of a New Nation", New York: Alfred A. Knoff, 2003.

Haile, Edward Wright "Jamestown Narratives: Eyewitness Accounts of the Virginia Colony: The First Decade: 1607-1617", Chaplain: Roundhouse, 1998.

Egloff, Keith and Deborah Woodward "First People: The Early Indians of Virginia" Charlottesville: The University Press of Virginia, 1992.

Wood, Karenne, Charlottesville: Virginia Foundation for the Humanities, 2007.

Kelso, William M. and Beverly Straube "Jamestown Rediscovery 1994-2004", Association for the Preservation of Virginia Antiquities, 2004.

William Nelson, Documents Relating To The Colonial History Of The State Of New Jersey, Vol. XXI, pg. 73, (Calendar of Records in the Office of the Secretary of State. 1614-1703), 1899

Butler, Jon. Awash in a Sea of Faith: Christianizing the American People. Cambridge, Mass.: Harvard University Press, 1990.

Rountree, Helen C. "Pocahontas, Opechancanough: Three Indian Lives Changed by Jamestown", University of Virginia Press: Charlottesville, 2005

Pascoe, F. C. Two Hundred Years of the S. P. G., 1701–1900: An Historical Account of the Society for the Propagation of Bible in Foreign Parts. London, 1901.

"Society for the Propagation of the Gospel in Foreign Parts (SPG)" (John Cannon, The Oxford Companion to British History), Oxford University Press

Butler, Jon. Awash in a Sea of Faith: Christianizing the American People. Cambridge, Mass.: Harvard University Press, 1990.

Robert Gray "A Good Speed To Virginia", London, 1609 Sydney King "A Diverse Jamestown Household 1620-1640", National Park Service, 2015

Howell Creative Group "William Strachey, Historic Jamestowne" Jamestown Rediscovery Foundation, 2021 Gannet, Henry "The Origin Of Certain Place Names In

United States, Second Edition" Department Of The Interior, Unites States Geological Survey, 1905

Britannica, T. Editors of Encyclopaedia. "Virginia Company." Encyclopedia Britannica, April 5, 2021.

Pascoe, F. C. Two Hundred Years of the S. P. G., 1701–1900: An Historical Account of the Society for the Propagation of Bible in Foreign Parts. London, 1901

Noah Webster's 1828 English Language Dictionary

"The Life of Benjamin Lundy" (Philadelphia, 1847), 16. The manuscript record is in the archives of the Ohio Historical and Philosophical Society

Letter On Colonization: Addressed To The Rev. Thornton J. Mills, Corresponding Secretary Of The Kentucky Colonization Society Volume No. 1. C.1

Indian Land Cessions: Land Claims by Tribe

American State Papers, Miscellaneous, II, 278, 279. The Petition reached Congress on January 18, 1816. It was referred to the Committee on the Public Lands and reported on adversely. Annals of Congress, 14th Cong., 1st session, 691

The Fourth Annual Report Of The Kentucky Colonization Society: With An Address, (Delivered At The Request Of The Society) Kentucky Colonization Society

More About The Author

More About The Author

Dane Calloway is an American educator, author, film editor, film writer, film producer, well-respected historian, and an unorthodox researcher with well over ten years of creditable experience specializing in ethnographic, field, and historical research in various categories such as American Indian history, World history, African-American history, American history, case studies and also investigative journalism.

Dane Calloway is the founder of Im Just Here To Make You Think Inc., in which he and his company specialize in providing unconventional educational writings and audiovisual works, by sharing knowledge of surreptitious information, that uncovers unembellished truths that are generally not mentioned and/or known to the public.

Dane prides himself on being a freethinker and motivates all people to gain the absolute will to deprogram themselves from traditional propagated methods of indoctrination, to take full ascendancy over their very own mindsets once again.

Hence his slogan – "I'm Just Here To Make You Think".

Im Just Here To Make You Think Inc. as a company closes the gap between what is a fact (opinion) or truth by detailing unconventional current and or historic information via documentation, historic artifacts, manuscript materials, video, and audio recordings, photographs, films, published books, letters, newspapers, scrapbooks, journals, archives, and other publications; Extracted from the world's absolute best sources of factual information, and some of the most costly but yet credible publicly verifiable evidence from all across the world.

We strive to provide the most accurate and meritorious details of information, not generally mentioned or yet known to the public, surrounding a variety of topics including American History, World History, American Indian History, Native American History, Genealogy, Law, National, and World News.

Our ultimate goal is fully embedded within our name #ImJustHereToMakeYouThink

Collect all Dane Calloway books at www imjusttheretomakeyouthink.com/books or anywhere books are sold:

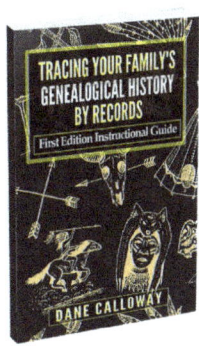 

Copyright © 2022 by Im Just Here To Make You Think Inc. and Dane Calloway and Taneisha Calloway. All rights reserved.

Published by Mr. & Mrs. Calloway Inc.
www.imjusttheretomakeyouthink.com